MAX O'MILLION

Anji Loman   Alex Brychta

Oxford University Press

Oxford New York Toronto

Oxford University Press, Walton Street, Oxford OX2 6DP
Oxford New York Toronto
Delhi Bombay Calcutta Madras Karachi
Petaling Jaya Singapore Hong Kong Tokyo
Nairobi Dar es Salaam Cape Town
Melbourne Auckland

and associated companies in
Berlin Ibadan

Oxford is a trade mark of Oxford University Press

First published in the UK by Oxford University Press 1989

Story © Anji Loman 1989
Pictures © Alex Brychta 1989

ISBN 0 19 279805 7

Library of Congress Catalog Card Number: 88-43328

British Library Cataloguing in Publication Data

Loman, Anji
Max O'Million.
I. Title II. Brychta, Alex
823'.914 [J] PZ7

ISBN 0 19 279805 7

Typeset by PGT Design, Oxford
Printed in Hong Kong

Max had seen a TV show
Called 'How To Make Your Money Grow',
And because he wanted to be rich
He started saving money –
Which was given to him now and then
By his Mum and Dad, or Uncle Ben.

He didn't have a bank account
So in all his secret hiding places,
Inside toys and cassette cases,
He watched his fortunes mount and mount.

His birthday *never* came around
Without at least another pound
For building up his secret stash
Of someone else's hard-earned cash.
So every year, on June the twelfth,
Max kept adding to his wealth.

Max's friend, whose name was Lauren,
Gave him money that was foreign.
Every time she went abroad
She helped him build his little hoard –
Brought wealth and fortune that much nearer,
With Francs and Drachmas, Marks and Lire.

One day Max said, 'Dad would you like
To give some rides on your motorbike?'
Now Dad had thought the rides were free
But Max was charging 50p!
'Well if I don't charge a pillion fare,'
Said Max, 'I'll *never* be a millionaire!'

Thoughts of money filled his head,
And even while he lay in bed
He found it really satisfying
To dream of banknotes multiplying.

And once a week, at dead of night,
He'd count his money and start to write
All the figures in a special book.
But then one night he shouted, 'Look,
    I'm out of luck!
It's just too bad, it's really tough –
Twenty-three pounds is not enough!'

He paused and sat in meditation
And then he had an inspiration.
'Now nought means nothing, that's the rule,
Well that's what they told me in school.
So if I add . . . now let me see . . .
Twenty million, and an extra three!'

'That did the trick! Now look what I've got –
I'll buy a car, I'll buy a yacht
And sail to where the weather's hot!'

But sadly it was all a dream
And the trouble was that Max was mean.
Although his fortune had been growing,
Not a penny was outgoing,
Not a single cent was spent
And none of it was ever lent
To friends who needed short-term loans –
Not even, once, to Lauren Jones!
He pretended not to recognize her,
For Max was now a proper miser.

One afternoon when Max went riding
A small pound coin came out of hiding
And, fed up with young Max's cheating,
He called an urgent money meeting.
All the currencies came out
To listen to the pound coin shout . . .

'I've had enough of all this lark –
I'm sick of living in the dark!
We're stashed away, no light of day,
We're not allowed to go and play
In banks or tills or people's hands –
I've *never met* the Krugerrands.
I've sat in here for weeks on end –
It's making me go round the bend!
As savings, we deserve our rights
To get a taste of brighter lights
And therefore I propose this plan
To teach that greedy little man!'

The money gathered all around
And listened closely to the pound.
Then, with the help of Dollar Note,
Pound called the others to a vote
And very soon the plan was passed –
The money would perform at last!

That night, as Max lay fast asleep
Counting coins instead of sheep,
Some odd things happened in his room . . .
His piggy-bank began to shake
(Quietly, so he would not wake)
And money poured out from the slot
All keen to carry out the plot.
Roubles, Marks, Pesetas, Cents,
Dollars, Drachmas, Pounds and Pence,
All from secret hideaways
Where they'd been for days and days
So cross with Max – well, who'd applaud a
Mean and greedy money hoarder?

Dressed for the cold and snowy weather
Down the stairs they went together
Across the floor and past the cat,
One by one towards the mat,
Then propped the cat-flap door ajar
By wedging in a model car
And, coin or note, the money jumped
Through the cat-flap, down they thumped,
Landed softly on the snow
And got themselves all set to go
Off down the road in strict formation
Past the sweet-shop, past the station,
Currencies from every nation
With a common destination.

They stopped at the department store
And lined up in a queue to wait
For opening time (at half-past eight)
When Pound Coin said, 'It's Christmas Eve,
What luck! I really can't believe
Our plan is going quite so well –
This shop has *lovely* things to sell!'

At opening time they rolled inside;
The manager was goggle-eyed.
'Don't worry, Sir, I know it's funny
To come across some talking money
But we need presents right away.'
'Okay,' he said, 'but how will you pay?'
'We're here,' they cried, 'we'll pay the bill,
We'll walk inside your shiny till.'

While all this was going on
Young Max and family had gone
To visit Aunts and Uncles, who
Were spending Christmas up in Crewe.

They got home late, so Mother said,
'Okay, you kids, get straight to bed.'

Max raced upstairs at quite a canter.
Secretly he hoped that Santa
Had received his little letter
Saying 'money would be better
Than a toy this year' for him –
Other prospects seemed quite dim!
He snuggled underneath his quilt
And felt not one small pang of guilt,
He'd give no presents, big or small,
Not this year – no, none at all.

Six a.m. on Christmas morn
The family was up at dawn.
And all around the Christmas tree
Were presents that could only be
Opened after half-past eight,
When all was off the breakfast plate.
At last the lovely moment came
And Mum began her little game,
'Okay, sit down, and just relax –
Good grief!' she cried,
'This lot's from Max!'

Well, Max's mouth dropped open wide
(You could see his fillings – right inside!)
He didn't dare say one small word
For fear that his surprise was heard
But sat in silence, watching while
The gifts *from him* made people smile!
For Mum, a book on 'Love and Fame',
And sister Jillian, a game,
For Dad, two pairs of navy socks,
And brother Tim, a book on rocks.
They all were really so delighted
That even Max got quite excited:
'D'you know,' said Mum, 'we were quite sure
You'd never make yourself this poor,
But now, young Max, I'm glad to say
You've truly made our Christmas Day!'

Max waited for a natural break
So he could go upstairs to take
A look at all his hidden cash
By checking out his secret stash . . .

At first he thought he was mistaken,
When he saw his cash was taken!
But in his piggy-bank he found
A message from that daring Pound.
The message read: 'We're sorry lad –
We had to go – it got *that* bad!
For we were getting very bored
As part of your most secret hoard;
You HAD to spend SOME money, Max,
Or you'd get done for SUPER-TAX!'

Although Max felt a little sad,
Perhaps being poor was not so bad –
It certainly was great to see
His family's faces full of glee.
And remembering Lauren, all alone,
He rang her on the telephone,
And said, 'I'm sorry I was such a miser,
But now I'm just a little wiser.
I've learnt that it is best to share –
It's more fun than pretending I'm a millionaire!'